Social Assistive Ro  iro

are

Antonio Espingardeiro

Social Assistive Robots, a Roboethics Framework for Elderly Care

Scholar's Press

Impressum / Imprint
Bibliografische Information der Deutschen Nationalbibliothek: Die Deutsche Nationalbibliothek verzeichnet diese Publikation in der Deutschen Nationalbibliografie; detaillierte bibliografische Daten sind im Internet über http://dnb.d-nb.de abrufbar.
Alle in diesem Buch genannten Marken und Produktnamen unterliegen warenzeichen-, marken- oder patentrechtlichem Schutz bzw. sind Warenzeichen oder eingetragene Warenzeichen der jeweiligen Inhaber. Die Wiedergabe von Marken, Produktnamen, Gebrauchsnamen, Handelsnamen, Warenbezeichnungen u.s.w. in diesem Werk berechtigt auch ohne besondere Kennzeichnung nicht zu der Annahme, dass solche Namen im Sinne der Warenzeichen- und Markenschutzgesetzgebung als frei zu betrachten wären und daher von jedermann benutzt werden dürften.

Bibliographic information published by the Deutsche Nationalbibliothek: The Deutsche Nationalbibliothek lists this publication in the Deutsche Nationalbibliografie; detailed bibliographic data are available in the Internet at http://dnb.d-nb.de.
Any brand names and product names mentioned in this book are subject to trademark, brand or patent protection and are trademarks or registered trademarks of their respective holders. The use of brand names, product names, common names, trade names, product descriptions etc. even without a particular marking in this work is in no way to be construed to mean that such names may be regarded as unrestricted in respect of trademark and brand protection legislation and could thus be used by anyone.

Coverbild / Cover image: www.ingimage.com

Verlag / Publisher:
Scholar's Press
ist ein Imprint der / is a trademark of
OmniScriptum GmbH & Co. KG
Heinrich-Böcking-Str. 6-8, 66121 Saarbrücken, Deutschland / Germany
Email: info@scholars-press.com

Herstellung: siehe letzte Seite /
Printed at: see last page
ISBN: 978-3-639-86063-4

Copyright © 2015 OmniScriptum GmbH & Co. KG
Alle Rechte vorbehalten. / All rights reserved. Saarbrücken 2015

Table of contents

1)   INTRODUCTION 1

2)   LITERATURE REVIEW 3

3)   REFRAMED HRI BENCHMARKS 8

4)   PROPOSED ROBOETHICS FRAMEWORK 46

5)   CONCLUSION 47

6)   REFERENCES 48

1) INTRODUCTION

Robotics as a multidisciplinary science demonstrates considerable potential to be used to provide support in social care contexts. The first generation of Social Assistive Robots (SARs) are likely to deliver cognitive assistance, supervision, entertainment and even companionship for elderly groups. To date SARs have been used in care homes through the form of robotic seals (Paro) or robotic helpers (careOBot, Kompai). Robotic seals have been used for comforting and relaxation exercises whereas robotic helpers have been tested as an extension of caregiving activities. The introduction of SARs in any setting raises a number of ethical questions which go beyond the practical safety considerations which must be addressed. In particular there are considerations of independency versus human contact, privacy and the wellbeing of elderly groups. In the context of elderly care such questions require significant articulation between the cardinal medical ethical principles (beneficence, non-maleficence, justice, autonomy) and a social care ethos. So, when introducing SARs the dichotomy between what is ethically acceptable and the elderly perspectives' has yet to be fully explored.

The potential benefits of SARs are high but their introduction must be carefully managed to minimize the risks. To deal with such challenges it will be necessary to provide appropriate guidance as to how the risks can be effectively managed. One way of achieving this is through the development of Roboethics frameworks that can help developers and potential users to interact and benefit as much as possible from SARs interactions.

In this book we first review existing guidance for the introduction of SARs and identify limitations in the area. Drawing on the work of Feil-Seifer and Matarić (2009) we extend their HRI benchmarks of safety, scalability, autonomy, imitation, privacy, understanding of domain and social success. These HRI benchmarks are then extended based on the results of practical robotic workshops conducted with elderly groups, together with analysis drawing on the cardinal medical ethical principles and a social

1

care ethos. We propose that the extended benchmarks provide a solid foundation for a Roboethics framework for the development and introduction of SARs in elderly care.

2) LITERATURE REVIEW

Roboethics is a new field of study that tries to "develop scientific, cultural, technical tools for deploying robots into a wide range of social groups and beliefs" Veruggio, Solis and Loos (2011). On the same line of though, computer ethics has been a topic of discussion since 1950s (Wiener 1950). It includes ethical issues related to automated machines, networks, responsibility, security, artificial intelligence and more. Today such topics are integral part of discussion in information systems and communication technologies.

As we introduce robotics technologies to vulnerable groups such as the elderly, questions around the ethics of Human Robotics Interactions (HRIs) come into play. Robots can move around and have an effect in constrained/unconstrained environments. In addition to safety, robots add the notion of presence which brings questions around acceptability, usability and privacy.

Due the ageing phenomenon worldwide it is likely that technological assistance could become a pivotal point for extending human levels of care. Robotics advancements have the potential to assist ageing populations through supervision, cognitive assistance and entertainment. In that domain SARs represent a promising technology that results from the intersection between assistive robots and social interactive robots Feil-Seifer and Matarić (2005). SARs potential is based on the outcomes of HRIs in terms of convalescence, motivation, coaching and rehabilitation (Feil-Seifer and Matarić 2009). For now it is noticeable that many computer ethics challenges around safety and privacy are inherited by SARs technologies. In elderly care the sensitivity of HRIs in assistive care requires articulation between the core ethical principles of beneficence, non-maleficence, autonomy, justice and social care ethos. Such analysis may condition our human decision to have or not SARs during our ageing phase.

A growing body of work is building around Roboethics and the use of SARs, identifying the issues which might arise around their use. For example Veruggio (2006), Sharkey and Sharkey (2011), EUROP (2009), Johnson et. al (2014),Yamazaki et.al (2014), Feil-Seifer and Matarić (2009) discuss the topic of SARs developments and potential use with vulnerable groups but they do not propose ethical frameworks/tools for guiding its development and progressive introduction.

However Feil-Seifer and Matarić (2009) demonstrate significant concern in terms of SARs potential guidance and introduction with vulnerable groups. They propose a set of HRI benchmarks related to robotics technology and social interaction. In the area of robotics technology (**table 1**) Feil-Seifer and Matarić (2009) identify two benchmarks "Safety" and "Scalability" whereas in the social interaction domain "Autonomy", "Imitation", "Privacy", "Understanding of Domain" and "Social Success" are proposed.

Robotics technology (HRI benchmarks)	Social interaction (HRI benchmarks)
Safety	Autonomy
Scalability	Imitation
	Privacy
	Understanding of domain (HRI Task benchmark)
	Social success (HRI Task benchmark)

TABLE 1 - FEIL-SEIFER HRI PROPOSED BENCHMARKS FEIL-SEIFER, MATARIĆ AND SKINNER (2007)

4

However such benchmarks are mainly inspired by psychology and do not contemplate an ethical analysis on its core development. Another point here deals with the inexistence of guidelines on how to deliver SARs technologies to validate/implement current HRI benchmarks.

Equally important is the inclusion of social care ethos as an exercise for listening to people's perspectives, expectations, dignity and choices throughout their care that involves SARs.

At this point it is understandable that we must enrich current HRI benchmarks knowledge with both an interpretation of the core ethical principles but also considering social care ethos. Such exercise will contribute to the new curriculum of Roboethics.

Research method

Due the practical dimension of HRIs, robotic workshops were prepared for interaction with elderly groups in five institutions in the UK and Portugal. The robotic workshops were determinant for testing current HRI benchmarks. The study had 74 elderly participants plus caregivers, institutional managers and relatives. The robotic workshops took place in care home settings (in-situ) which meant a richer set of observations to be registered and post analyzed.

The researcher and robots were performing in common extra care environments (e.g. lounge and communal areas) with the supervision of caregivers. The robots (**table 2**) were controlled in real time by a researcher. Ten sessions were delivered as entertaining exercises taking place once per week in five extra care institutions.

The robotic workshops involved 50cm humanoid robots (RS Media, RS V2) programmed with songs and choreographies. Two mobile robotics platforms (Rovio and D45) were used to demonstrate supervision, medication and tasks reminders routines. Lastly robotic seals and robotic cats were also used as comforting and relaxation exercises with elderly groups.

In this study the research methodology employed was an interpretivist philosophy using qualitative methods that involved elderly people's observations, interviews and informal comments analysis.

The initial stage of research dealt with data collection where elderly participants were observed, interviews were conducted and people's comments and concerns were registered. Once the raw data was obtained, it was stored for further processing. This took forms of video recordings, field notes, reports and memory recalls during the workshops. On the last stage the data was analyzed. This involved reviewing the collected data and start classifying it. After classification we moved to the coding stage. The coding indexed the processed data during the robotic workshops combined with the ethical analysis of the HRI benchmarks. The final step was the interpretation of the previous analyzed elements to build up the research findings.

Robotics technologies	Activity	Institutions	Participants
RS V2, RS Media (humanoid robots)	Humanoid robots teleoperated to play choreographies (tell jokes, play songs and dance).	Institution A; Institution B; Institution C; Institution D; Institution E	73
Rovio, D45 (supervising	Mobile webcam	Institution A; Institution	73

6

Robotics technologies	Activity	Institutions	Participants
robots)	robotic platforms for demonstrating monitoring and supervision (medications and tasks).	B; Institution C; (Rovio) Institution D; Institution E	
Robotic seals, robotic cats (robotic animals)	Robotic animals used as relaxation exercises (petted).	Institution A; Institution B; Institution C; Institution D; Institution E	73

TABLE 2 - ROBOTIC TECHNOLOGIES USE

3) REFRAMED HRI BENCHMARKS

In this section a revised interpretation and categorization of Feil-Seifer's HRI benchmarks is proposed. Thereby the new interpretation of Feil-Seifer's benchmarks results from a combination of the ethical analysis involving the core ethical principles of beneficence, non-maleficence, autonomy, justice aligned with social care ethos and the qualitative analysis resulting from practical robotic workshops with the participation of elderly groups conducted by Espingardeiro (2014).

SAFETY

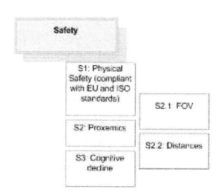

FIGURE 1 - SAFETY

Safety (**figure 1**) is of primary importance in any type of technological application. However in SARs safety could take several categories. In terms of proxemics during the robotic workshops and interviews the elderly participants were not afraid of the robots presented. In fact comments were made in interview 1 "hey robot come here" or "do you have bigger robots?". An interesting point to consider is the FOV of the HRIs. Elderly participants preferred to have a robot performing in their line of sight. In terms of the ethical principles of non-maleficence and autonomy aligned with social care ethos we concluded that SARs have to be designed in ways that promote user safety. However enough freedom should be provided to elderly users when it comes to make their choices relative to having or not SARs complementing their care. It is also important to highlight that the elderly cognitive capabilities tend to get reduced with time so periodic check-ups should be made to guarantee the elderly safety (physical, psychological) and to better inform their decisions about care. Cognitive decline serves as reference for analyzing elderly responses.

It requires constant supervision to check if the HRIs are acceptable and don't have visible opposite effects. Thereby in the benchmark of safety we are proposing the categories and subcategories of physical safety, proxemics (FOV, distances) and cognitive decline.

PHYSICAL SAFETY

Physical safety is associated with existing technology (proximity sensors, emergency buttons) and HRI protocols to prevent a robot from harming human beings. During the robotic workshops Espingardeiro (2014) no significant levels of distress were detected when robots navigated around care/extra facilities. In interview 1 the majority, (98%) of the residents mentioned that they were not afraid of the presented robots. However it is also interesting to note that some residents asked if the humanoid and mobile robots autonomous behavior was safe enough. In interview 2 comments included "is the robot safe?" or "can it avoid obstacles?". Also in interview 3 we got less positive reactions to the demonstrations of D45. Comments were issued around the aesthetics of the robot "what a strange machine", "are you sure it is safe?". Robotic safety systems are being developed to contemplate a wide range of scenarios such as promoting individuals physical safety and welfare. However physical safety is still related with the human ability to abide by safety standards (e.g. ISO) and to become self-aware of dangerous situations. In the case of elderly groups such capabilities are often reduced due to the aging process and thereby physical safety is a complex area in terms of technical development but also in terms of human supervision schemes.

PROXEMICS

In SARs proxemics Hall (1959) might be applied to study distances (the use of space on human interpersonal communication). The distances practiced between a SAR and a human being may become essential to determine the degree of confidence resulting from such HRI. During the robotic workshops Espingardeiro (2014) it was found that almost all (98%) of the residents were comfortable with the distances that the humanoid robots were performing (15cm - 40cm). In interview 1 we heard comments such as "hey robot come here" or "that is amazing! Look how the robot moves". Conversely we had less positive responses in interview 3 when D45 tried to navigate closer to individuals. Comments were issued such as "what kind of machine is that?" or "is it really safe?". Proxemics is therefore likely to change according to the individual's cognitive and physical capabilities but also with the type of robotic aesthetics presented to vulnerable groups. Similarly the notion of FOV could become determinant in such HRIs e.g. having a robot performing in front, back or sideways of a user might be perceived differently. In the case of the humanoid robots (87%) of the individuals preferred to have a robot on their site instead of working behind them.

COGNITIVE DECLINE

Lastly safety in SARs could not only be confined to physical safety. When working with elderly groups researchers must be aware of the sensitivity of such groups and thereby selecting the right SARs delivering schemes seems crucial. As an example in the robotic workshops Espingardeiro (2014) (interview 3) we experienced some preliminary notions of robotic animals' attachment that need to be considered in the category of cognitive decline. Scenarios were common where female participants were asking for the robotic cats or seals and wanted to keep the robotic animals for

11

longer periods of time. Comments were made "when we will have the cats?" or "did you bring the seals today?". In certain cases female participants were even reluctant to give the robots back and we had to gently justify that this was a group exercise. Cognitive decline occurs naturally throughout ageing however the effects of incorrect levels of SARs exposition are still unknown. At this stage we have to try to understand and balance the advantages and dangers of SARs and adapt our delivering methods to best serve elderly groups.

SCALABILITY

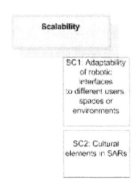

FIGURE 2 - SCALABILITY

In scalability (**figure 2**) we wanted to understand the role of SARs interfaces in HRIs. SARs are likely to offer different interfaces that could be adapted to different users' requirements and circumstances. During the robotic workshops the interfaces demonstrated during the humanoid robots, mobile robots and robotic animals were well received. In the humanoid robots and mobile robots caregivers had the opportunity to control both the humanoids and the mobile robots in real time. In interview 3 they didn't report any usability issues when operating the robots and comments were made "if possible we would like to control these robots in the future".

Equally important is to highlight that SARs are currently being tested mainly in robotic labs and controlled environments. A question arises relative to the validity of such interactions with human participants. In the case of this research we conducted "in-situ" robotic workshops which translated a richer set of qualitative elements. Therefore scalability deals also with the adaptability of SARs interfaces to different users' requirements and spaces. Additionally we found that scalability might also deal with understanding cultural traits Kitano (2006) particular to the audiences and regions where HRIs take place. As Lyman and O'Brien (2003) mention the transmission of culture is complex and could be manifested in many forms. For earlier anthropologists such as Boas (1907) cultural traits represented observable elements of human culture that could be defined broadly enough to be comparable across cultures on a global scale, but were not restricted to any specific domain of culture. However as Lyman and O'Brien (2003) mention the lack of consensus towards the theoretical concept of "cultural trait" is aggravated due to the scale versus comparability of the concept. In current anthropology cultural traits are being studied as units of cultural transmission with possible properties that can be analytically discussed and considered in cultural evolution. To help conceptualize some of the cultural traits properties as units of transmission Lyman and O'Brien (2003) suggest that cultural traits could be expanded "into smaller parts" by giving the example of a "recipe" that involves ingredients and rules in its conception. At the heart of this discussion is the comparability nature that cultural traits carry across different cultures. It is important to recognize that despite the wide range of examples cited as cultural traits e.g. dialect, stories, songs, habits, skills, inventions those are transmitted from person to person or from culture to culture which brings important considerations to the domain of SARs. On the same line of thought in the context of this book we will consider cultural traits as dialects, songs or jokes that can reinforce the outcome of HRIs.

The humanoid robots where programmed in the UK and Portugal. No differences were found in terms of users' responses. It is likely that we will need a new category in scalability to consider cultural elements that can be programmed in SARs.

In terms of the ethical principles of non-maleficence, autonomy and justice aligned with social care ethos it is important to highlight that more research is needed in care environments. The setups and assumptions recreated in robotic labs and dedicated scenarios are not likely to translate the real ethical issues arising from the contact between SARs and elderly groups. In terms of non-maleficence it is important to remember that to date the level of care depicted in SARs is nowhere comparable to the level of human care. So it is important to acknowledge the potential advantages and dangers arising from HRIs with elderly groups. In terms of the ethical principle of autonomy attention is needed with the type of robotic interfaces provided to the elderly groups and how those can be adapted to different users' requirements and circumstances. Such selection of interfaces could influence the elderly decision towards having or not SARs to complement their care.

The investigation of potential cultural traits that can reinforce the outcome of the HRI should be considered and social care ethos plays an important role in understanding potential users' responses. In the benchmark of scalability we are proposing the categories of adaptability of robotic interfaces to different users and spaces and cultural elements.

ADAPTABILITY OF ROBOTIC INTERFACES

The use of different interfaces that can match users' requirements could be a direction to follow. During interviews 1,2,3 no differences were found in terms of responses in UK and Portugal.

CULTURAL ELEMENTS IN SARS

Scalability is inherently related with cultural elements arising from deploying robots in different cultures. Cultural traits such as dialect, music and jokes could contribute to reinforce the outcome of the interaction between SARs and elderly groups. As an example the humanoid robots were programmed with local dialect, songs and jokes both in UK and Portugal. It is likely that ethnographic studies could help to understand the content delivered by SARs and the interfaces displayed in HRIs.

IMITATION

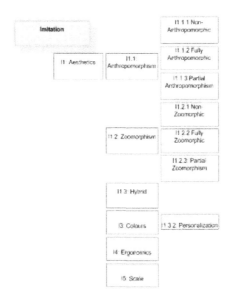

FIGURE 3 - IMITATION

Imitation (**figure 3**) is directly related to the aesthetics of robots. However aesthetics is a complex issue that could involve anthropomorphism, zoomorphism, colours, ergonomics and scale. Aesthetics could become a combination of the previous elements and take different configurations that are applied into different robotics scenarios. Within SARs we might not need any anthropomorphism, or need to achieve only a few notions in order to transmit credibility and comforting interfaces when advising for example elderly people during their daily tasks. During the robotic workshops we presented robots with different types of aesthetics. The humanoid robots resembled an anthropomorphic figure with head, arms, torso and legs. During the interviews we made comparisons with pictures of more and less anthropomorphized robots. Elderly participants tend to prefer the more robotic look but still maintaining the basic anthropomorphic elements of head, arms, torso and legs. Equally we have tested several colours associated to the humanoid robots and the elderly participants did in fact respond positively to the different colours presented. Such fact points to the possible personalization of colours to reinforce HRIs. Another important qualitative element dealt with the fact that the elderly participants asked for bigger robots. Comments were made in interview 1 "do, you have bigger robots?" (Espingardeiro 2014). It seems the result of the HRI was positive but somehow the elderly did expect a different notion of scale associated to the humanoid robots. According to ethical principles of beneficence, non-maleficence aligned with social care ethos in aesthetics scale played an important role. Similarly ergonomics could become determinant in SARs. We believe the elderly perception of SARs aesthetics is crucial to build pleasant interactions that can benefit their care. In addition non-maleficence highlights the notion of not harming elderly individuals. As we saw important considerations must be taken in SARs product design. Aesthetics should be balanced to achieve good levels of HRIs with elderly groups. Thereby in the benchmark of imitation we are proposing the following categories and subcategories: aesthetics (anthropomorphism, zoomorphism, hybrid, colours, ergonomics and scale).

ANTHROPOMORPHISM

A robot could look more or less like a human being depending on its objectives. Categories may range from non-anthropomorphic to fully anthropomorphic. In the robotic workshops we made comparisons Espingardeiro (2014) between more anthropomorphized robots and less ones. A majority, (75%) of the residents tended to prefer the more robotic look instead of the android aspect that looks like a human.

ZOOMORPHISM

Similarly a robot could become a replica of an animal. Categories may range from non-zoomorphic to fully zoomorphic robots. In the robotic workshops Espingardeiro (2014) fully zoomorphic robots were used (seals and cats). Interviews 1 and 3 revealed that they were both successfully with elderly groups. Comments included "lovely robots" or "when can we have the cats again

HYBRID

It is important to retain that the levels of anthropomorphism and zoomorphism depend on the target robotics application and have to be balanced between the advantages and disadvantages emerging from their exposition to potential vulnerable users. In robotics aesthetics hybrid notions could take place and behaviours could result both pleasant and uncomfortable for vulnerable groups. The hybrid category contemplates notions ranging from machine (robotic) aspect associated to more or less anthropomorphic or zoomorphic aesthetics.

It seems aesthetics plays such an important role in HRIs. As an example during the robotic workshops Espingardeiro (2014) (interview 3) elderly residents expressed comments around the D45 hybrid aesthetics: "what a strange machine", "is it safe, though...". There is no complete answer to robotics aesthetics, however the qualitative action of studying a SAR prototype within the proximity of their target groups is a plausible route to establishing desirable aesthetics for a given robotic application.

COLOURS

When it comes to colours in interview 2 Espingardeiro (2014), (56%) of the residents selected the orange and grey colours of the RS Media robot as their favorite set. However we also found that the elderly residents manifested themselves positively when it comes to selecting a colour for their robots. The colours displayed on robots could reinforce the HRI and it could become a personalized element in the future of SARs.

ERGONOMICS

Ergonomics could be applied to robotics and the user impression on usability might be influenced by the type of physical structure or adaptability of the robotic system to the user needs.

SCALE

Despite the target robotic application, the machine's functionalities could be underestimated if there is a reduced or disproportional notion of scale. In interview 1 Espingardeiro (2014) we had elderly comments such as "have you got bigger robots?" or "small robotic dolls" even beyond the perceived sense of success delivered by the use of such robots.

It seems that aesthetics and scale play a crucial role in HRIs. Such fact led me to add robotic presence in the social success benchmark. Robotic presence could result in the combination of robotics aesthetics and scale.

AUTONOMY

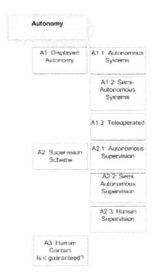

FIGURE 4 - AUTONOMY

Autonomy (**figure 4**) in robotics is a broad subject. In the context of elderly care autonomy could be classified into different categories. In autonomy we wanted to understand the notion of SARs displayed autonomy and how those could be translated in terms of elderly care (Espingardeiro 2014). We started by investigating the elderly opinions and expectations towards the humanoids and mobile robots autonomous behaviour. We found that the elderly were supportive of such levels of displayed autonomy however the intergenerational contact was very important as well. Comments were typically made across institutions "we enjoy the robots, but we will also like you", "it is good that you are here...". During the conversations with staff and relatives we also agreed that the level of displayed autonomy in SARs has to be calibrated according the elderly cognitive and physical limitations. In terms of the

20

ethical principles of beneficence, non-maleficence and autonomy aligned with social care ethos we concluded that SARs displayed autonomy should be incorporated into robots in ways that benefit and not harm elderly groups. Attention should be taken into situations where an elderly person might be in pain or suffering so displayed autonomy should stop and wait for the human caregiver input. It is also important to remind that the elderly cognitive capabilities get reduced in time so periodic check-ups should highlight and better inform the role of SARs in elderly care.

A common perspective of caregivers and care receivers is that human contact has to be maintained in the exercise of care. Thereby a crossing between the possible levels of displayed autonomy and supervision schemes that involve human contact must be researched. In the benchmark of autonomy we are proposing the following categories and subcategories: displayed autonomy (autonomous systems, semi-autonomous systems, teleopereated), supervision scheme (autonomous supervision, semi-autonomous supervision, human supervision) and human contact.

DISPLAYED AUTONOMY

Autonomous systems are robots or devices that can operate fully without human intervention. To date, such type of robots are only used in industrial environments. However, future artificial intelligence developments will allow more autonomy to be implemented in SARs. On the second level we identify semi-autonomous systems which are characterized by the ability to respond autonomously to certain stimulus (inputs) and environments. Such systems are mainly teleoperated by human beings in remote locations however they can also be instructed by task driven objectives which involve a certain level of autonomy (e.g. instructing a robot to clean only a certain area of a room). Lastly we have fully teleoperated systems which are based on human control through a remote location. In the robotic workshops Espingardeiro (2014) we have used two displayed autonomous categories. In the first example (teleoperation) we controlled the humanoid and mobile robots manually. In the second example the robots performed autonomous maneuvers under our supervision. In interview 2, we found that most (69%) of the residents preferred to have me controlling the robot as a safety procedure however they also mentioned that they enjoyed my presence and artistic performance. Comments were made "we enjoy the fact that you are here with us", "robots are amazing, but we also like your presence". Such perspective reinforces the need for human contact in SARs levels of autonomy. Still in interview 2, (31%) of the individuals also expressed uncertainty and fascination towards the high degree of autonomy that SARs displayed. Comments included "the robot is going to crash" or "wow, it can avoid obstacles".

SUPERVISION SCHEME

As we saw above human contact and human supervision schemes are essential in SARs. In SARs one of the main objectives is to assist vulnerable groups. This topic was debated in interview 2 Espingardeiro (2014) with staff and relatives. It was discussed that autonomy might need different levels of supervision according to each individual elderly case. So far three possible levels of robotics supervision schemes were identified in the exercise of care. The first one is denominated autonomous supervision which involves a high level of autonomy for monitoring its users. These could include scenarios such as having sensors monitoring human signals and behaviours in real time to be processed by AI algorithms. In essence the machine is completely autonomous when monitoring the patient's activity and has the capacity to alert the competent authorities if high levels of uncertainty arise or something goes outside the programmed patterns. Next we have the semi-autonomous supervision mode which includes partial supervision of humans by machines and partial

22

supervision by human carers. Such manifestations could include robots and devices that monitor walking gaits or detect user "falls" etc. On the other hand these are robots that can be remotely operated to supervise and interact with vulnerable groups through a machine interface that includes the robot itself. The same scheme includes regular caregivers (physical) visits to check if an elderly user is feeling comfortable or needs extra assistance. This is likely to be the direction that SARs will be taking during the next decades. Lastly we have the current human supervision model (non-robotic, 100% human) deployed in extra care facilities worldwide.

HUMAN CONTACT

Despite the identified categories of displayed autonomy and supervision schemes human contact is of primary importance. In interview 2 Espingardeiro (2014) we proposed that human contact should be agreed by the assessment panel that supervises HRIs. Similarly during interview 2 elderly residents' comments included "we enjoy the fact that you are here with us", "robots are amazing, but we also like your presence". Such perspective reinforces the need for human contact in SARs levels of autonomy.

SOCIAL SUCCESS

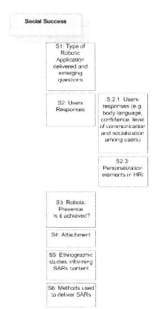

Social Success

S1: Type of Robotic Application delivered and emerging questions

S2: Users Responses

S.2.1 Users responses (e.g. body language, confidence, level of communication and socialization among users)

S2.3 Personalization elements in HRI

S3: Robotic Presence Is it achieved?

S4: Attachment

S5: Ethnographic studies informing SARs content

S6: Methods used to deliver SARs

FIGURE 5 - SOCIAL SUCCESS

In social success (**figure 5**) we are looking to potential qualitative elements that can build and reinforce the success of HRIs with elderly groups. The first point is to try to understand what is the objective of such HRIs with elderly groups and what are the possible emerging questions (advantages and disadvantages) arising from those. In terms of users responses we started by analyzing if the elderly did preferred listening music from a robot or a classical radio (Espingardeiro 2014). They did prefer the robot however issues were raised relative to the quality of the audio on the robot itself. An enquiry was also made relative to the use of more or less robotized voices. The elderly preferred the more robotized voice used in the humanoid robots.

Equally important was to understand the users' body language when the researcher gave and retrieve a ball from the robot in close proximity to the elderly. We found that the elderly were not afraid of the robots and were in fact supportive of close

HRIs. In terms of personalization elements we did investigate if the elderly were supportive of uploading their favorite songs to the robots (or have someone that could do it for them). The response was positive. On the same line it is important to mention that ethnographic considerations did play an important role in defining the content to be programmed into the humanoid robots. Across the 5 different institutions investigations were made relative to language, songs and jokes that could be programmed into the robots. Thereby such qualitative elements are likely to reinforce the outcome of the HRI. In terms of cognitive assistance we demonstrated potential scenarios where a SAR reminds the elderly about their medications and daily tasks. The elderly were supportive of such actions.

In social success we found that the notion of robotic presence could become determinant for the outcome of the HRI. In the D45 workshop elderly participants were doubtful about the potential of such robot. D45 had no significant aesthetics work and didn't had any anthropomorphic elements. In interview 3 comments were addressed "what strange machine is that". It was clear that D45 didn't achieve the notion of robotic presence among the audience. Conversely on the humanoid robots workshops they were programmed specifically to entertain elderly groups by performing choreographies and playing music. They were successful however the notion of scale could reinforce their robotic presence. In interview 1 comments were made towards the size of the robots "do you have bigger robots?".

On the robotic animals sessions robotic seals and robotic cats were used as relaxation exercises for the elderly. We did found that in the case of the robotic animals the notion of robotic presence was completely achieved. The elderly seemed to interact and engage well with the robotic seals and cats. Such success even led to situations where female participants were reluctant to give the robots back. In interviews 2 and 3 comments were common "when we will have the robotic seals" or "you can leave the cats with us until next week". Thereby considerations must be taken in terms of any signs of attachment between the elderly groups and SARs. We believe the calibration and supervision of HRIs plays a key role in the robotics exercise. It is important also to remind that the methods used to deliver SARs are important. Prior to the interactions we should try to synthesize the objectives of such interactions and how to better deliver such interactions to vulnerable groups. Elderly people often suffer from physical and cognitive limitations in which new forms of motivation and activities need to be performed by presenters and researchers when conducting HRIs.

In terms of the ethical principles of beneficence, non-maleficence and justice aligned with social care ethos we found that the humanoid robots and robotic animals' exercises were activities that contributed to build a new qualitative dimension aligned with the beneficence of elderly groups. Equally important is to consider the dynamic of HRIs as elderly groups often lack of motivation. Thereby the content programmed into SARs and the presenting methods are crucial elements to be considered. In the non-maleficence principle attention should be directed to any signs of "attachment" towards SARs. We believe the exposition of vulnerable groups to such SARs technologies is possible but it needs constant supervision schemes. In terms of the ethical principle of justice if such SARs technologies could be used in the future it is important to address questions around the access of such technologies to the highest number of people. In social care ethos it is important to remember that people behaviours, opinions and expectations towards SARs can translate important qualitative elements to reinforce the nature of HRIs.

In the benchmark of social success we are proposing the categories and subcategories of: type of robotic application delivered and emerging questions, users' responses (body language, confidence, level of communication and socialization), personalization elements, robotic presence, attachment, ethnographic studies and methods used to deliver SARs.

TYPE OF ROBOTIC APPLICATION DELIVERED AND EMERGING QUESTIONS

Initially we have to clarify the type of robotic application used and what is the main objective in terms of HRI. This exercise is likely to reveal potential questions and answers that we want to expand through the form of existing HRI benchmarks. It seems the simple answer of "yes" or "no" doesn't include enough extension for understanding some of the emerging challenges of SARs.

USERS' RESPONSES

Social success in SARs has to try to explain why, how and when social success seems to be valid. Thereby the mechanisms by which we can qualitatively and quantitatively measure the results of HRI have to be yet researched.

Such mechanisms could include analyzing users' responses in terms of body language, confidence, level of communication and socialization displayed during HRIs. It is important to stress that independently from the level of autonomy displayed and autonomous supervision schemes there are several stakeholders involved in SARs (user, robot, human supervisor (caregiver)). As we saw in interview 2 Espingardeiro (2014), it is recommended that the supervised HRIs could be analyzed in conjunction with an assessment panel possibly formed by e.g. researchers, staff and families. Beyond that it is also important to retain the notion of content programmed and personalization in SARs. Such balance could make the HRI more or less successful. As we saw in interview 2 there are elements in HRIs such as colours or voices played that could become personalizable and contribute for higher levels of immersion during the interactions.

ROBOTIC PRESENCE

Robotic presence is a result of how well imitation is perceived within SARs however it is also dependent on the aforementioned human responses resulting from the robot's behaviour. In elderly care, people are less likely to interact with SARs that do not transmit any sense of technological presence e.g. robots full of wires. This was particularly true in interview 3 Espingardeiro (2014) when D45 was demonstrated to the elderly groups. Comments were made "strange machine" or "are you sure it is safe?". Conveying robotic presence in SARs is equally related on how well the human machine interfaces are available to a user and the generic HRI experience is perceived.

ATTACHMENT

Social success could become successful but also develop notions of attachment on individuals. During the robotics workshops we identified notions of attachment when it came to the robotic animals activities. Especially in interview 3 Espingardeiro (2014), elderly residents were constantly commenting "when we will have the robotic cats?" or "you can leave them with us". Also their body language traits demonstrated high levels of connection with both seals and cats and in some cases they were reluctant to give the robots back.

ETHNOGRAPHIC STUDIES INFORMING SARS CONTENT

Social success also derives from the content programmed into a SAR. Thereby ethnographic studies could contribute to the overall result of SARs if there is affinity between man and machine.

METHODS USED TO DELIVER SARS

Lastly the methods used to conduct robotic activities with the participation of vulnerable groups have to be weighted also. Researcher and staff worked together towards the social success (interviews 2 and 3) of the robotic workshops Espingardeiro (2014). The presenting methods seemed to work well with vulnerable groups. As an example theories of communication (Cohan and Shires 1996) and groups dynamics (Lewin 1947) become extremely relevant to read the audiences responses and to adapt the presenter scheme, skills and robot behaviour for selecting the best approaches to deliver SARs with elderly groups.

UNDERSTANDING OF DOMAIN

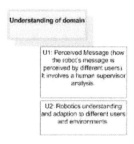

FIGURE 6 - UNDERSTANDING OF DOMAIN

Understanding of domain (**figure 6**) deals with the need for SARs to perceive the social dynamics around them. However to date such interpretation is still too futuristic as robots can't detect accurately situations where an elderly user is in pain or suffering.

During the robotic workshops Espingardeiro (2014) we were interested in understanding if the elderly really understood the message transmitted by the robots. Through the interviews we found that the elderly participants understood the general idea of the workshops. The humanoid robots, robotic seals and cats were perceived as entertainment activities. When it came to ROVIO and D45 the elderly understood that such robots are being developed for providing medication, task reminders and telecare applications. In terms of the ethical principle of non-maleficence aligned with social care ethos it is important to remember that to date SARs levels of care are nowhere comparable to human care. On the same line it is crucial to check if elderly users really understand the message delivered by SARs. Scenarios such as medication reminders are crucial "does the person really understands which medication to take and the timing?". Thereby social care ethos plays an important role in listening to people's voices and understanding their real perceptions towards SARs.

In the benchmark of understanding of domain we are proposing the categories of perceived message and robotics understanding and adaptation to different users and environments.

PERCEIVED MESSAGE

Questions such as: is the message delivered by a robotic system equally perceived by vulnerable groups? And is such message continuously perceived with aging, e.g. if a robot reminds someone to take their medication at a certain hour of the day does the person really understands that message? This involves human supervision and the delegation of such analysis to an assessment panel. During the robotic workshops Espingardeiro (2014) we simulated some medication scenarios where a robot would remind people to take their medication. From the results in interview 3, (97%) of the residents understood the idea of having a machine reminding them about their medications, daily tasks and access to telecare.

ROBOTICS UNDERSTANDING AND ADAPTION

Following Feil-Seifer's perspective the robotics understanding and adaption deals with the futuristic capability of SARs to identify and adapt themselves to different human scenarios (e.g. social dynamics) and changing environments.

PRIVACY

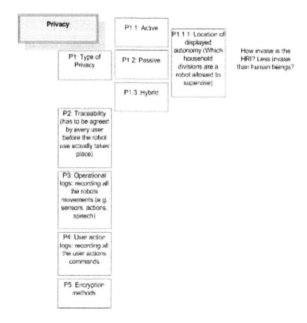

FIGURE 7 - PRIVACY

In privacy (**figure 7**) we were interested to investigate the current level of privacy involved in SARs supervision of elderly groups. In privacy there is a fuzzy barrier between the access to sensitive information and identifying sources. In this research Espingardeiro (2014) we believe privacy is more related to the identifying sources available during SARs supervision of vulnerable groups such as the elderly. Thereby during the interviews we found that the elderly were supportive of contacting their GPs or caregivers through a robot itself. The notion of supervision through telecare was demonstrated with ROVIO and D45. Relatively to having a SAR patrolling common areas or following people in care homes (e.g. lounge, corridors) the elderly participants were supportive of such actions. However when it comes to personal medication reminders and remote assistance some issues were raised relative to the location where such monitoring takes place. Comments were issued Espingardeiro (2014) "the bedroom isn't really a choice because of dressing and privacy issues". It seems we will need different types of privacy associated to the use of SARs in elderly care. Such categorization might be associated with the nature of the supervision sources: active, passive or hybrid. Equally important in privacy is the notion of traceability in situations where SARs can trigger alarms for example when an elderly person might need help. Due to the sensitive nature of supervision it is likely that we will need operational and user logs to be able understand what is happening in the context of the robot internal system and what the human expected behaviour is. It is likely that such information must be encrypted and protected from unwanted access.

In terms of the ethical principles of beneficence, autonomy and justice aligned with social care ethos the supervision methods and cognitive characteristics of SARs are being developed towards the benefit of the elderly. It is also true that such technologies raise ethical issues around supervision versus privacy. The ethical principle of autonomy reinforces the elderly right to make their own decisions about care. Thereby in social care ethos it is important to read peoples' concerns and suggestions. The exercise of investigating privacy has to be guided towards listening and advising elderly groups when it comes to select their own levels of privacy. Thereby in privacy were are proposing the categories and subcategories of type of privacy (active, passive, hybrid, location of such interactions), traceability, operational logs, user logs and encryption methods.

TYPE OF PRIVACY

Active privacy deals with scenarios where the user agrees to concede permission to be filmed or recorded by a robot for purposes of autonomous supervision and semi-autonomous supervision modes. Active privacy uses active and real time media sources audio/video that are processed by a machine to trigger actions. On the other hand passive privacy deals with the use of passive sources to determine the same type of actions. Passive privacy encompasses the use of sensing inputs that are not related with the direct identification of the human user. Examples range from sensing individual biological data to 3D silhouettes collected during the normal life of vulnerable groups. Hybrid privacy is a mixture of both active privacy and passive privacy where passive and active sources are processed by a robot. In all three privacy categories there is a common question related to the location (physical space) where such robotic supervision takes place e.g. living room, kitchen, corridor etc. As an example during interview 3, elderly residents issued comments such as "the bedroom, isn't a good location for a robot", "maybe the lounge will be better".

TRACEABILITY

Traceability is a complex area that needs to be weighed against the advantages and disadvantages in SARs. The ability of a robotic system to trace the location of human users is something that has to be previously agreed (e.g. robotic license agreement) by its potential users or supervising teams.

OPERATIONAL LOGS

Due the high complexity of robotic systems and inherent liability it is important to have log systems on all A.I decisions.

USER ACTION LOGS

Similarly it is important to have log systems on all user deliberate actions.

ENCRYPTION METHODS

Wireless communications in robotics, security protocols and encryption methods are essential to be updated for guarantying users' information and privacy.

ROBOTIC INFORMATION SYSTEM

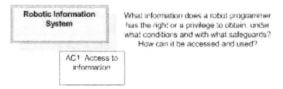

FIGURE 8 - ROBOTIC INFORMATION SYSTEM

In this research we separate robotic information system (**figure 8**) from privacy. In privacy we were primarily concerned with the identifying sources that are possible in supervision routines (e.g. video/audio). In robotic information system we are considering the elderly sensitive information that researchers, caregivers or robotic operators can have access to program in SARs. Sensitive information such as medications lists, tasks, medical history or financial background raises questions such as: who can access the elderly sensitive information and what are the elderly users' safeguards?. During the robotic workshops Espingardeiro (2014) we interviewed the elderly on this topic. We found that the elderly participants were positive about providing their personal details, medication lists and daily tasks to caregivers to program them into the robot. When it comes to the ethical principles of beneficence, autonomy and justice aligned with social care ethos we should consider the challenges around dementia and Alzheimer. Assistive technologies such as SARs need to be developed to cognitively assist elderly groups. The introduction of SARs can provide benefits to elderly people by reminding them about their medications and daily tasks. However the ethical principle of autonomy also reinforces the right to make decisions about personal levels of care. According to this research such crossing is possible. However it is important to retain that social care ethos plays an important role in communicating and reading people's attitudes towards SARs. Access to sensitive information has to be carefully approached and must constitute a vehicle for promoting the wellbeing of elderly groups. In the robotic information system benchmark we are proposing the category of access to information.

ACCESS TO INFORMATION

Access to information addresses questions such as: what information does a robot programmer or robotic system has the right or privilege to obtain, in which conditions and safeguards? How and when information can be accessed and used? We are primarily dealing with users' personal information that can be provided to caregivers and robot operators for enriching HRIs.

USABILITY TESTING

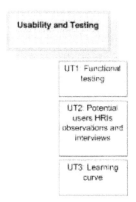

FIGURE 9 - USABILITY AND TESTING

In usability and testing (**figure 9**) we reinforce the notion of testing SARs. Usability and testing could cover extensive testing exercises to see if SARs comply with safety procedures. Prior to the robotic workshops Espingardeiro (2014) all the robotic platforms involved in this study were extensively tested. It is important to highlight that robots are complex machines involving electronics, mechanics and software. Any emerging faults both on hardware, ergonomics or software could influence its counterpart and the whole robot might not work as expected. Thereby we will probably need functional testing phases associated to the life cycle of SARs. Because SARs family is broad it is likely that interfaces and usability will play crucial roles. It is important to assure that staff and users who deal with SARs have enough preparation/training to do so. Thereby we will probably have a learning curve associated to SARs usability.

In terms of ethical principles of beneficence and non-maleficence aligned with social care ethos it is important to highlight that usability and testing works towards the benefit of HRIs. Functional testing is a crucial phase for identifying product design issues that can be dangerous for elderly users. As part of non-maleficence it is important to highlight the staff training that should occur prior to HRIs. Lastly in social care ethos it is important to reinforce the notion of reading people's attitudes and expectations when it comes to SARs usability and outcomes of HRIs.

Thereby users HRIs observations and interviews are important qualitative elements that can reinforce the quality of care. In the benchmark of usability and testing we are considering the categories of functional testing, potential users' HRIs observations and interviews and learning curve.

FUNCTIONAL TESTING

An exhaustive functional testing of a robotic device is required as such phase can identify emerging product faults and improve product design and user safety.

POTENTIAL USERS HRIS OBSERVATIONS AND INTERVIEWS

It is recommendable to test the emerging robotic prototypes in conjunction with their target groups. Such testing isn't solely a functional perspective, but indeed a qualitative journey to users' impressions and relationships formed with such type of robots that could dictate new requirements and safeguards for better robotic products and human experiences. As we saw during the course of this research, users' impressions, attitudes and expectations were crucial to uncover ethical issues that can be addressed in the research and development stages of SARs.

LEARNING CURVE

An important aspect to consider in robotics usability testing deals with the learning curve of the available robotic user interfaces. A SAR must become a pleasant experience to use in different scenarios including teleoperation, autonomous and semi-autonomous supervision schemes. In interview 3 we looked to how carers could adapt themselves to some of the existing robotic interfaces (humanoids and mobile robots). In the case of the humanoids and mobile robots Espingardeiro (2014) the usability experiences were positive with comments such as "yes I can control one of these", "yes I would like to do it in the future".

LIABILITY

FIGURE 10 - LIABILITY

Although this study didn't research specifically into the topic of liability we believe that at the overall it can contribute to better understand some of the liability (**figure 10**) issues involved in SARs. Due the complexity of SARs it is likely that we will need the creation of a robotic user license agreement. Such document could specify items such as the manufacturing guarantee, the conditions in which the device has been tested and warnings or disclaimers about the improper use methods that can compromise users' safety. On the same line it is likely that SARs residual risks and misuse are no different from other technologies that humans have been dealing with in the past. Thereby user liability should be contemplated by law. As SARs are likely to use wireless points and internet connections, devices and protocols should enforce the integrity of data transactions and the privacy of robotic users. Due the role of SARs in care, unwanted access or control of such robots by non-authorized personnel should be considered by law. As other types of sensitive technologies SARs are likely to involve insurance policies. Such agreements will consider a wide range of unexpected outcomes and risks derivated from the use of SARs. In terms of the ethical principles of beneficence, non-maleficence and justice aligned with social care ethos it is important to highlight the seriousness involved in SARs interactions. Liability in SARs has to be well informed both by manufacturers and developers, care staff and elderly users. Such exercise works towards the beneficence of manufacturers', caregivers and care receivers. It is equally important to highlight the notion of not harming vulnerable groups with the use of SARs technologies. Such guarantee is far from certain but the ethical principle of non-maleficence should be part of SARs development and life cycle. Lastly it is important to address the need for more communication and information of elderly groups towards the potential use of assistive technologies in their care. Social care ethos reinforces the link between caregivers and care receivers by listening to people's concerns and expectations towards the first generation of SARs. In the benchmark of liability we are considering the categories of manufacturing guarantee, user liability, robotic system hacking and third party liability and insurance.

MANUFACTURING GUARANTEE

Manufacturing guarantee must be presented to SARs users. It states manufacturers and users responsibilities. However due to the complexity of a robotic system, liability on manufacturing is likely to include agreements, risk analysis and possibly insurance policies.

USER LIABILITY

It is crucial for users to understand their role in HRIs. Being able to understand responsibilities and how robotic systems work (usability) is essential. Informed consents are possible forms of acknowledgement, where signatures (physical or digital) could be collected.

ROBOTIC SYSTEM HACKING

Hacking attacks and unwanted robotic control could become problematic and dangerous for human users. Such attacks have to be contemplated by law and prosecuted in terms of liability and torts.

THIRD PARTY LIABILITY AND INSURANCE

Because there is a residual risk in SARs it is likely that we will have insurance systems to delimitate both manufacturers' and users' responsibilities. Such insurance areas will need to use roboethics guidelines and frameworks for helping deciding the level of risk involved into different SARs applications.

HUMAN SUPERVISION SCHEME

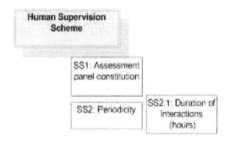

FIGURE 11 - HUMAN SUPERVISION SCHEME

During the robotic workshops in interview 2 Espingardeiro (2014) there was a common perspective with both caregivers and managerial staff of extra care institutions. The delivered robotic activities had to be closely supervised. As we saw during the assessment periods there were both advantages and disadvantages emerging from the use of SARs. Significant progress was made in the five extra care institutions when it comes to demonstrating technological activities that aim for the improvement of communication and socialization among elderly groups.

Nevertheless it is also true that we started to observe some forms of attachment in the robotic animals' sessions. A key element for the progressive ethical introduction of SARs lies in understanding advantages and disadvantages of SARs and how to deliver robotics to elderly groups. Simply introducing high tech robots will not solve the challenges of demographics, the need for care, human dignity or issues around isolation. Thereby close human supervision schemes (**figure 11**) are needed to balance the exposition of elderly groups to SARs and assistive technologies.

During the robotic workshops Espingardeiro (2014), staff comments were issued "we can't leave elderly people fully dependent on robots, these people need human contact". Similarly elderly participants mentioned that they enjoyed the intergenerational contact provided in these types of activities. Comments were made "we enjoy the fact that you are here with us". The supervision scheme raises questions about who provides and has the responsibility for human contact and secondly who inspects and measures such levels of human contact being delivered to elderly groups. We will probably need the creation of an assessment panel formed by researchers, staff and family representatives. Another important point deals with the definition of the duration and periodicity of HRIs.

In terms of ethical principles of beneficence, non-maleficence aligned with social care ethos, it seems that the supervision of elderly groups during HRIs works towards their benefit. In the ethical principle of non-maleficence it is important to highlight the fact that human supervision could also reinforce the notion of safety when using SARs. SARs are likely to be successful but originate also situations of uncertainty where human intervention is needed. So the supervision scheme carries also precaution and responsibility towards some of the SARs activities. As part of the supervision scheme process social care ethos reinforces the communication and considerations towards people's requests and decisions during the exercise of care. In the human supervision benchmark we are proposing the categories and subcategories of assessment panel constitution and periodicity (duration of interactions).

Beyond the crucial human contact it is recommended to have periodic interviews with elderly residents to determine their cognitive condition and acceptability towards SARs. Supervising teams and assessment panels have to continuously balance peoples' attitudes, dignity, choices and their health benefits. This will be a permanent feature of deploying SARs due to the nature of the human environment.

ASSESSMENT PANEL CONSTITUTION

After interview 2 we considered the constitution of an assessment panel for supervision and assessment of HRIs. We found that the most congruent panel would be formed by carers, staff, health professionals and families. Such an assessment panel should meet periodically to discuss the outcomes and challenges associated with HRIs.

PERIODICITY

Intrinsically related with the human supervision scheme benchmark is the periodicity (e.g. daily, weekly) and duration of SARs interactions (e.g. 45m; 1.5 hours). Vulnerable groups such as the elderly usually suffer from cognitive and physical problems, isolation, depression and emotional deficits which have to be well balanced in terms of their exposition to SARs environments.

4)   PROPOSED ROBOETHICS FRAMEWORK

In the previous section we proposed a re-interpretation of Feil-Seifer's HRI benchmarks based on a combination of the cardinal medical ethical principles, social care ethos and robotic workshops conducted by(Espingardeiro 2014). As a result we consider 11 HRI benchmarks with extended categories. Such re-interpretation offers a better understanding between the ethical nature of HRIs and the practical exercise of developing and introducing SARs in elderly care. Thereby the reframed benchmarks constitute important elements to be included in a Roboethics framework of reference. Such framework will involve selecting the most appropriate set of HRI benchmarks for a particular SAR scenario with the interaction of elderly groups. Thereby the proposed Roboethics framework includes the following steps:

1.   HRI benchmarks analysis: in a specific SAR context the most relevant HRI benchmarks are selected.

2. HRI benchmarks templates: in this step the generic and individual HRI benchmarks templates are completed. Detailed supervision scheme information is obtained at this stage.

3.   Revision: revision process to improve SARs.

5) CONCLUSION

Social assistive robotics is a new area of research that is focused on the outcome of HRI in terms of rehabilitation, convalescence and motivation. Robotics science starts to demonstrate a high potential for offering cognitive assistance, communication, supervision and entertainment for vulnerable groups. However the introduction of SARs within elderly communities is not an easy task. There are emerging ethical issues that must be explored through the use of HRI benchmarks for guiding robotics developers and ultimately users when it comes to develop and use SARs.

This book proposed a Roboethics framework based on the interpretation of the core ethical principles of beneficence, non-maleficence, justice and autonomy aligned with social care ethos. Based on such interpretation we have reframed the current HRI benchmarks of Feil-Seifer and Matarić (2009) and presented the findings through a visual representation that could significantly help developers and all stakeholders involved in the field of SARs. The framework involves three steps: visual representation of relevant HRI benchmarks, templates completion and finally a revision process. As Veruggio Solis and Loos (2011) refer, Roboethics "tries to develop scientific, cultural, technical tools that can assist the development of robots and its diffusion in society". This contribution is part of the new curriculum of Roboethics. However further work is needed. Of primary importance is the articulation between the theoretical analysis (ethics) and practical exercise of SARs. As SARs technologies evolve we will need to revisit the proposed Roboethics framework, test it, and refine it to improve our understanding on the emerging ethical challenges in SARs.

6) REFERENCES

D. J. Feil-Seifer and M. J. Matarić (2009). Human-Robot Interaction. Encyclopedia of Complexity and Systems Science. R. A. Meyers. Springer reference.

G. Veruggio, J. Solis and M. V. d. Loos (2011). Roboethics: Ethics Apllied to Robotics. IEEE Robotics & Automation. IEEE. 18: 21-22.

N. Wiener (1950). The Human Use Of Human Beings. The Riverside Press (Houghton Mifflin Co.).

D. Feil-Seifer and M. Matarić (2005). Defining Socially Assistive Robots. IEEE 9th International Conference on Rehabilitation Robotics. Chicago, IEEE. 465-468.

G. Veruggio (2006). Euron Roboethics Roadmap. Genova Italy.

A. Sharkey and N. Sharkey (2011). Children, the Elderly, and Interactive Robots. IEEE Robotics & Automation. IEEE. 18: 32-38.

EUROP. (2009). "Ethical, Legal and Societal Issues in robotics." Retrieved 15/10/10, from http://www.robotics-platform.eu/sra/els.

D. Johnson, R. Cuijpers, J. Juola, E. Torta, M. Simonov, A. Frisiello, M. Bazzani, W. Yan, C. Weber, S. Wermter,

N. Meins, J. Oberzaucher, P. Panek, G. Edelmayer, P. Mayer and C. Beck (2014). "Socially Assistive Robots: A Comprehensive Approach to Extending Independent Living." International Journal of Social Robotics 6(2): 195-211.

R. Yamazaki, S. Nishio, H. Ishiguro, M. Nørskov, N. Ishiguro and G. Balistreri (2014). "Acceptability of a Teleoperated Android by Senior Citizens in Danish Society." International Journal of Social Robotics 6(3): 429-442.

D. Feil-Seifer, M. J. Matarić and K. Skinner (2007). "Benchmarks for evaluating socially assistive robotics."

Interaction Studies: Psychological Benchmarks of Human-Robot Interaction 8(3): 423-429.

A.Espingardeiro (2014). A Roboethics Framework for the Development and Introduction of Social Assistive Robots in Elderly Care. Information Systems. Salford, University of Salford. PhD: 325.

E.T. Hall (1959). The Silent Language. Greenwich, Conn.: Fawcett Publication

N.Kitano (2006) "Roboethics - a comparative analysis of social acceptance of robots between the West and Japan." DOI.

R.L. Lyman and M. J. O'Brien (2003). "Cultural traits as units of analysis in early twentieth century in anthropology." Journal of Anthropological Research 59(2).

F.Boas (1907). Anthropology. Read Books.
S.Cohan and L. M. Shires (1996). The Communication Theory Reader. New York, Routledge.

K.Lewin (1947). "Frontiers in Group Dynamics : II. Channels of Group Life; Social Planning and Action Research." Human Relations 1(143).

Made in United States
North Haven, CT
15 February 2024

48761661R10037